HOW NOT TO GET DIVORCED

Powerful Principles to Help You Prevent Divorce
and Have a Happier Marriage

Michael Caputo

HOW NOT TO GET DIVORCED

Copyright © 2016 Michael Caputo

ISBN-13: 978-1537660592

ISBN-10: 1537660594

To Leonilda: my precious wife, unparalleled mother and great contributor to our marital success.

Michael Caputo

DISCLAIMER: This book is designed to provide information and motivation to our readers. No warranties or guarantees are expressed or implied by the author's choice to include any of the content in this book. Neither the publisher nor the individual author shall be liable for any physical, psychological, emotional, financial, or commercial damages, including, but not limited to, special, incidental, consequential or other damages.

ACKNOWLEDGMENTS

My views toward the sanctity of marriage were shaped by God and Jesus Christ's teachings as found in the Holy Scriptures. The deepest gratitude, first and foremost, goes to them. Many have been the authors and ministers who have taught me many wonderful principles, over the years. The list would be too long to include in this section. My parents and my in laws' example of unwavering commitment to their marital union has been a priceless reference point when marital challenges came our way. I also want to thank my children for their love and especially my wife, Leonilda, who has contributed a vast amount to building our special relationship.

TABLE OF CONTENTS

PREFACE

INTRODUCTION

1: WE HUMAN BEINGS HATE REALITY.

2. WE HUMANS ARE ESSENTIALLY SELFISH.

3. HUMAN BEINGS HAVE A TENDENCY TO BE FILLED WITH PRIDE.

4. RECOGNIZING LIMITS IN OURSELVES WILL MAKE US MORE PATIENT WITH OTHERS.

5. YES, LOVE CAN DO WONDERS.

6. REALISTS WILL INHERIT THE EARTH.

7. AFFAIRS DO NOT ADD SPICE TO A MARRIAGE.

8. FINANCIAL STRESSES CAN BE RESOLVED WITH PATIENCE AND RESOURCEFULNESS.

9. YOUR MATE MAY NOT NECESSARILY BE A BAD PERSON.

10. IT MAY NOT BE LAZINESS, IT MAY BE....

11. IT IS OK TO BE JEALOUS BUT...

12. RIGIDITY IS THE ROYAL WAY TO TROUBLE.

13. SPICE UP YOUR SEX LIFE — BUT NOT WITH PORNOGRAPHY.

14. LISTENING: A POWERFUL TOOL.

15. NAME CALLING: A LETHAL WEAPON.

16. AFFECTION: THE HEALING BALM.

17. GRATITUDE: THE ENERGIZER.

18. DON'T BELIEVE EVERYTHING YOU SEE.

19. BEWARE OF BITTER FRIENDS.

20. REMEMBER: YOUR CHILDREN ARE WATCHING AND LEARNING.

21. GIVE HONEY BEFORE CORRECTION.

22. PRAY DAILY FOR YOUR MATE.

23. SUPPORT YOUR MATE PUBLICLY.

24. SUPPORT YOUR MATE IN FRONT OF YOUR CHILDREN.

25. BE THE SOOTHING BALM, AFTER A STRESSFUL DAY.

26. MASSAGES ARE A TOKEN OF LOVE.

27. RESPECT THE DIFFERENCES.

28. PUT YOUR MATE ON A VERY HIGH PEDESTAL.

29. LOVE YOUR MATE AS LIFE TRANSFORMS HIM/HER.

30. BE A PILLAR OF STRENGTH FOR YOUR MATE WHEN DEATH TAKES LOVED ONES AWAY.

31. DIVORCE WILL NOT NECESSARILY SOLVE YOUR PROBLEMS.

CONCLUSION

ADDENDUMS

ADULTERY: A WORK OF THE FLESH

LOVE: A FRUIT OF THE SPIRIT

PREFACE

I am a psychotherapist and a family counselor. I have a bachelor of Psychology, a Masters' degree in counseling and a specialist in guidance counseling. I have taught Psychology at the College level, part-time, for 16 years. I have also done pastoral counseling since 1985.

I have the professional qualifications to write this book, but one thing qualifies me most of all: I married my wife, Leonilda, in 1979, and we are still together today, in 2016. We have raised three special children; we have gone through some very rough times financially; we have had many disagreements. We, at times, were temporarily angry at each other. In spite of the challenging times, we always emerged as best friends and are still very much in love.

My 37 years of marriage and of counseling various couples has helped me learn a lot about the challenges couples face. I have understood many things about women, about men and about the challenging human nature we have in common. In this book, I want to share what I learned with as many couples as possible, with the hope that some relationships may be affected for the better and that at least a few painful divorces might be prevented.

INTRODUCTION

In marriages we can find ourselves in a negative or a positive cycle. These cycles may begin gradually or suddenly, as a result of comments or actions by ourselves or our mate. The comments /actions are followed by responses from the one across from us, which can be positive, negative or neutral. Positive or neutral responses prevent negative cycles from beginning; negative responses can lead to negative cycles, deterioration and a downward spiral.

There isn't too much we can do about our mate's response, but there is *much* we can do about *our* words and actions.

If you are contemplating a divorce, you are

clearly in a negative cycle. You have spiraled down and now things are, or seem to be, out of control.

But that cycle can be broken. You have the capacity to bring the negative cycle to an end, by not adding anymore to it, and by sowing positive seeds which can lead you and your mate back into a positive cycle.

In this book you will be helped to gain insights about yourself and how you may be adding to the negative cycle you and your mate may be in. I will also give you principles which can and will bring back a positive cycle in your relationship—if used consistently.

All I ask of you is to have an open mind and to be willing to try some basic suggestions which have been proven to do wonders in relationships.

I believe that much can be done to salvage your

marriage. I understand that you may have tried other books and perhaps counselors, in vain. Please give it one more chance, and may you find in this book some answers that will bring harmony and love back into your relationship.

Most of all, may the following pages be a tool in God's hands to help you succeed.

1. WE HUMAN BEINGS TEND TO HATE REALITY

I hate reality; you most probably hate reality too. Humans beings tend to hate reality. The reality we hate the most is the fact that we are far from perfect, and that we have faults that frustrate, irritate and, at times, plain turn off others—especially our mates.

When our mate corrects us, we will fight back and we will do our utmost to rationalize our faults away. We will then proceed to point out to our mate that they may have the same plus other faults. This is typical. I have done it, and so has my wife — and that is a big mistake, especially when the fault that is being spotlighted affects the other person severely. If our habit creates a lot of irritation in our mate to the point that he or she starts crying, or starts yelling, or becomes depressed and discouraged, or it leads to heavy-duty cursing, then we have a problem.

We humans are a problem. In fact we are a set of various problems glued together by life. Thinking otherwise is self-deception. We humans have some severe problems that we love to deny. These problems may very well be the causes that are tearing your marriage apart, and they need to be confronted.

2. WE HUMANS ARE ESSENTIALLY SELFISH

We humans are selfish since childhood. This is one of the glaring traits of human nature. Our natural selfishness explodes during the teen years, and should start decreasing somewhat when we become young adults. In some of us the decrease is tangible, in some others it is barely noticeable.

We all bring selfishness into our marriage. We are all longing to be loved more than we long to love. We all long to have our needs met more than we long to meet the needs of our mate.

The first thing we need to face up to is the fact that selfishness resides in us. We need to admit to ourselves that it is there and that it refuses to relent.

Where are you in this? How selfish are you? Only you can answer this question, and you must do so honestly.

Please take your time; there is no need to hurry. You need to meditate on this, and you need to look back at the many times when you were less than altruistic. Then think about how many times your mate has called you "selfish." If she/he has done this often, beware: the problem may be more serious than you think.

3. WE HUMAN BEINGS HAVE A TENDENCY TO BE FILLED WITH PRIDE

I have pride in me; you have pride in you. The symptoms are several. Let's look at some manifestations of pride.

Sometimes people are plain inconsiderate, and our ego gets pinched. That is normal. It is OK to have a healthy self-esteem. Yet, if we get offended easily, and if we become defensive easily, that could be a sign that we might have a problem with pride.

King Solomon, my favorite wise man of all times, tells us that it is an honor to pass over offences

(Proverbs 19:11). A proud person will not pass over offences. A proud person will stew over offences. A very proud person will react to offences. An exceptionally proud person will want to get back at the source of offences, and a super-proud person will kill you over offences.

If you continually store hurts for future use, you may have a serious problem with pride. Where do you fit in all this? Look at the above reactions and ponder; consider where *you* are toward your mate.

Again, you may need to ponder for awhile, and if the problem is there, admit *to yourself* where you stand in this regard.

4. RECOGNIZING LIMITS IN OURSELVES WILL MAKE US MORE PATIENT WITH OTHERS

People who recognize that they are far from perfect will be more patient with others' imperfections. It is impossible to be harsh with others who show frailties, when we recognize that we also have frailties. The less we are willing to look in our mirror, the more we will be intolerant of others.

People who accuse others and who love to find faults in others, tend to be blind about themselves, as Jesus warned long ago. "Hypocrite! First remove the plank from your own eye, and then you will see clearly to remove the speck from your brother's eye" (Matthew 7:3 NIV).

If we enter a relationship with a self-righteous attitude, and we stay with a self-righteous attitude, we will contribute to an inevitable disaster.

Are we self-righteous? Do we tend to look outward *a lot*—but not inward? Do we see few faults, or worse still, do we see no faults at all in ourselves? Then we have a problem—a serious problem.

People who think they are perfect, or close to it, also think they have the right to judge, and criticize and condemn others. That is the royal way to turning people off—*to turning a mate off*.

It's time to ponder this principle as well, and if present (and it takes guts to admit it) it's time to admit it to *ourselves*.

5. YES, LOVE CAN DO WONDERS!

Once we realize that we are frail and faulty, then we need to check our love meter. Are we loving people? I am not saying, "are you in love?" That is a question that carries problems. In a marriage there are times when things are so overwhelming; when life is so stressful; when friction is so intense that you do not feel the kind of mushy love toward your mate that the question implies. The question I want to stress is, instead, "are you loving?"

If you are loving, you will be loving even when there are disagreements; when there are arguments; when the stresses of life will push you to the edge. You can love the other person even when problems abound—and yet not feel any of the mushy feelings that you may have felt when you first *fell in love*.

True love is other-oriented. True love really "bears all things" (I Cor. 13:7 KJV). Tue love bears the irritability of the other person; the quirks of the other person; the, at times, insensitivities of the other person.

Love is much greater than all the problems that come along, *and it can do wonders*. Selfishness, on the other hand, bears little—<u>and demands much</u>. Now it's up to you to decide if this problem resides in you — not in your mate — but <u>in you</u>.

6. REALISTS WILL INHERIT THE EARTH

When your eyes met your mate's eyes for the first time; when you felt bliss every time you were with your mate and started thinking that being with that person across from you would have meant bliss for life, you were in a state of unreality. In other words, *you were dreaming*!

Life with another person is not a decades-long dream; it is a series of challenges that test us at times to our limits, and will determine what we are made of; whether we are steel or mush; whether we are smoke or substance. Certainly, good relationships will have lots of tender moments and some, or many blissful moments; but expecting tenderness and bliss to frame the relationship *at all times* is a sign of a mind that refuses to see the light.

But you have a choice: you can either accept this undeniable reality, or you will add to an inevitable failure in your relationship.

Accepting reality brings peace to our minds; refusing to accept the truths of life will lead to frustration and depression.

I am being honest with you: there is no *ongoing* bliss in this world. Even drugs and alcohol, which promise such bliss and which some have foolishly embraced, will give you temporary relief and then the inevitable depression that follows and, finally, the inevitable self-destruction.

7. AFFAIRS <u>DO NOT</u> ADD SPICE TO A MARRIAGE

Some have actually tried it, and have lived to regret it, even if they got away with it for some time. Some such people actually fool themselves into thinking that they will grow in appreciation of their mates by experiencing sexual bliss with someone else. Who do they have in mind when they make love with their mates? Get the point?

Sex is supposed to create a blissful association with one's mate. It creates and strengthens a powerful bond. How can you bond with your wife, while bonding with someone else?

"Your sin will find you out," the Bible assures us in Numbers 32:23 (KJV). I have known of people who thought they could evade this powerful law —and did so for some time — *and then the unexpected crash!*

Years ago, I counseled a woman who had betrayed her husband for some years. She was finally found out by her teen-age son who, as a result, had a nervous breakdown and to cope with the pain went into heavy drugs. The woman's bliss soon turned into a nightmare. By the way, the lover left her and moved on to greener pastures, not long after.

Don't ever be fooled by devilish articles in popular magazines, or on the Internet, that adultery adds anything to your life. Adultery is a great evil, and it will bring you great pain — mentally, and at times physically, thanks to the viruses you will catch from the Don Juans, or the easy women who are often infected by incurable diseases that they caught from other lovers that they will callously share with you.

Never forget that people who are easy with you have gone to bed with other people who are also easy, who in turn have gone to bed with other people who are easy, who may have inherited destructive diseases that have been traveling and mutating from easy people to easy people for millennia. Is that what you want in your body?

And don't be fooled that condoms give you "safe sex." If condoms are only effective in preventing pregnancy four out of five times, how effective do you think they are in preventing STD's?

If you are interested in the Biblical perspective on adultery, please read the addendum on the topic later on in this book. It will spotlight the evils of adultery, and it will offer preventative principles, as well.

8. FINANCIAL STRESSES CAN BE RESOLVED WITH PATIENCE AND RESOURCEFULNESS

The biggest cause to marriage breakdowns is financial stress. Things get tough, at times; I know. About 20 years ago my wife and I went through some rough financial times — but we survived, and twenty years later we are now doing quite well.

All it takes is a recession — which by the way come our way, like clockwork, every 10 to 15 years. And when recessions hit, jobs are lost, businesses shut down, anxiety goes sky high— *and marriages fall apart.*

Yet, when we got married, most of us promised to stay together and to remain supportive even in bad times. Remember? "In good times and in bad times." Why? Because for most human beings there will be both.

It's easy to be supportive when things are good; that takes no commitment nor character. It is the crucible of bad times that tests our mettle — that tests what we are made of, if we are really committed to the other person or not.

Bad times *will come,* for many. When they do come, do we panic? Do we become resentful? Do we blame, or do we come together to come up with solutions?

Bad times will go. Yes, bad times tend to have a beginning and an end — *if we are patient, and resourceful.* Recessions come and go. The economy does finally improve. Bills will get paid—again. The mortgage will finally be paid off.

But even in this we have to be honest with ourselves. There are times when we are in bad financial shape because of factors we had nothing to do with. There are times when <u>we</u> are the cause of our financial stresses.

Did we overextend ourselves? Did we spend irresponsibly without considering the impact the debts would have had on us and on our family? Did we ignore the impact that it would have had on our relationship?

It's time, again, to admit. It's time to change, to be responsible, to sacrifice. It's time to start anew with a new outlook. It's time to be resourceful and be patient *together*—for better times *will* come again.

9. YOUR MATE MAY NOT NECESSARILY BE A BAD PERSON

Some people are difficult. Some people are hard to deal with. For some the reason is just plain selfishness; for some it may be pride; for some it may be both.

There are people, though, that are moody, irritable, impatient, snappy, easily angered and just plain explosive, most or all the time.

For quite a few, the cause is not simply lack of self-control or insensitivity; the cause is physical.

The person beside you may be "impossible" because of chemical imbalances in his/her body. We all know about the monthly period; we all know about menopause, and we may think that chemical or hormonal imbalances are a female monopoly. But that is not the case. Men can also have chemical imbalances that can make them irritable, moody, snappy and easily angered. Here are some:

a. **Low blood sugar, otherwise known as**

hypoglycemia.

This problem is very common and is more serious in some than others. We all have tasted the effects of low blood sugar. 2-3 hours after we eat, our sugar level drops, and that's when we become hungry and irritable. Or lunch time comes; the last meal was breakfast at 7 am. Our stomach growls and so do our minds. That is low blood sugar. *The brain is starving* and we become *very* irritable; except that some people have it worse than others and, therefore, become more irritable than others. Some become *beasts*. You or your mate could have this problem and don't even realize it.

I read about this condition, for the first time, many years ago in a book written by Judge T. Blaine titled *Mental Health Through Nutrition*. Judge Blaine was so convinced that low blood sugar was a big cause of irritability — and thus marriage discord — that he ordered couples that came to him to divorce to have their sugar levels tested.

I agree with Judge Blaine. There are way too many couples who fight regularly, and low blood sugar may be a cause—or <u>the</u> cause.

The best way to check is to be tested—but beware: regular blood tests don't necessarily show if there is a problem. You may need a test that lasts at least three hours, known as the Glucose Tolerance Test, so as to see what happens after a meal.

In the meantime, go on the Internet and research, "Low Blood Sugar" or "Hypoglycemia." This may totally transform your view of yourself, your view of your mate and may help save your marriage.

b. Vitamin and mineral deficiencies.

Do you have a poor diet? Are you into fast foods? Do you skip your fruits and vegetables? If so, you may have vitamin and mineral deficiencies. One deficiency that comes from not eating vegetables is a vitamin B deficiency.

If you have such a deficiency, as you can quickly check on the Internet, you will experience a variety of psychological symptoms—and one of them is irritability.

Calcium deficiencies can also lead to irritability. Your doctor can test you for this as well as hypoglycemia. Don't neglect asking for a test.

c. A high caffeine consumption.

Oh coffee...how good it is—*and how addictive*! And who can ever blame coffee for any harm, when studies are continually telling us about the many benefits. Of course, they never tell you that some such studies may have been financed by the coffee companies, nor will they tell you of other studies from reputable sources that may indicate that for some people coffee is downright harmful.

If you tend to be irritable, coffee will NOT relax you. <u>Coffee is a stimulant</u>. Most people will not be affected adversely; some will be turned into *impossible* human beings.

One person I counseled years ago — who was a walking bomb — drank 30 cups of coffee a day. His poor wife was living with a dangerous man. Nothing could be done about his explosive personality, until he remedied that problem.

You may simply become *somewhat* more irritable, because of coffee. Well, that is enough reason to stop. Have a *herbal* tea instead.

And by the way, regular tea is also a stimulant and chocolate, colas and some sodas may have caffeine in them as well. Beware! The caffeine in these drinks may be making you hard to live with, but this is a problem that can be remedied very quickly. Consider...

d. Allergies — to the environment and to foods.

Allergies abound. We all know the classic symptoms: watery eyes, sneezing, runny nose...but there is more. Allergies can make you fatigued, depressed — <u>and very negative and irritable</u> — and most people have no idea that they are having psychological symptoms because of allergies and/or food sensitivities.

When allergy seasons hit, pay attention to your irritability level. You may be surprised.

What about foods? Lots of people have sensitivities to common foods—and don't even realize it. They know, though, that, at times unannounced, they feel depressed or irritable, or may have mental fogginess for no known reason.

Well, there is a reason. It may be one or more of the foods you may have just eaten, and they could be the most common foods: wheat, sugar, milk products, corn, eggs or any other common food—and alcoholic drinks. Yes, some people are made irritable by alcohol—small amounts of alcohol. Could you be one such person?

Trust me, there is a lot of mental illness out there caused by sensitivities to foods— *common foods*. And you could be affected by them as well.

I won't stay with this point for long. If you want to know more, just go on the Internet and type "cerebral Allergies," or "food sensitivities" or "mental health and nutrition." You will be amazed at what you will find.

10. IT MAY NOT BE LAZINESS, IT MAY BE....

One of the complaints I heard over the years from unhappy married people is that the mate over time had become lazy. Unlike the past when the mate came home and quickly got to work to prepare a sumptuous meal or to mow the lawn, or fix things around the house, over the years the mate had become "lazy" and things didn't get done any more as they used to be.

The other person is seen as spending a lot of time on the couch, allowing things to deteriorate, while the husband or wife is watching frustrated and in disbelief.

No doubt, there are lazy people around. No doubt there are insensitive and irresponsible people around as well. But if the person was responsible for years and suddenly he/she appears to be so no longer, you may be dealing with more than just laziness and irresponsibility. You may be dealing with a physical or mental health issue, and, therefore, judging, blaming, accusing or even threatening would be the worst thing you could ever do.

There are millions of people in this world who have seen themselves go from being dynamic and responsible to feeling always fatigued and even depressed.

Please do not despair! And please do not even think of leaving your mate because he/she is not the person he/she used to be.

A few years ago a relative of mine entered such

a phase and the cause was adrenal fatigue because she was working too hard and was under too much stress and her adrenals stopped performing. She had to take a six-month-long leave from work and was restored back to normal.

Another person I know who was very dynamic and very responsible started slowing down dramatically and could not do the things he had to do to maintain the house. He looked lazy—but he wasn't lazy. After months of testing, it was found that his immune system was on overdrive and was using up his energy resources leaving him chronically exhausted. He is on now on the mend.

And then there are people with thyroid problems, deficiencies, low blood sugar and diabetes, and a host of other problems that may be sapping the person of energy, as well.

If tests don't seem to get to the root of the cause, that is not necessarily evidence that the person is lazy; it may simply be evidence that the cause has yet to be found.

And don't forget depression. Depression may be caused by all kinds of physical and/or psychological factors. One thing that <u>will not</u> help a depressed person any is calling the person "lazy" or threatening that if he/she will not "smarten up," you will leave the relationship. That will serve to push the other person over the edge—and nothing else.

Most of all, you will lose the other person's respect, and you are liable to create great resentment that will not be easy to heal.

11. IT IS OK TO BE JEALOUS, BUT...

Are you a jealous person? Most people are;

some mildly; some obsessively. The causes can be several. Some people are jealous because of insecurity. Some people are jealous, because they have been made insecure. Some people are jealous for good reasons.

Some people expect the mate to see them flirting with others and feel nothing. Yeah right!

Some people have been made insecure by betrayal, or hints of betrayal.

Some people are jealous because they themselves are up to no good, and they project their misdeeds onto their innocent mate. The problem is not the mate; the problem is *themselves*. Jealousy, in a way, is their mental punishment for betraying.

If the problem in your mate is insecurity due to betrayal of a parent who cheated on the other parent, you need to understand the cause and be patient, and do your best not to give reasons to cause jealousy. *You need to be extra patient and extra loving, in other words.*

If you are projecting your own faults, then your jealousy is a warning sign. Stop your actions and reap the positive consequence: peace of mind.

12. RIGIDITY IS THE ROYAL WAY TO TROUBLE

Some people are very easy going, others are very rigid, intolerant and uptight. Rigid people have one way of looking at reality and accept no other—*and respect no other*. There is no gray for such people, only black and white.

Some such people are religious extremists. They can make life a living hell for their mates and their children.

Such people tend to be legalistic and very rigid in

their expectations. They have no place for mercy in their world. They are harsh critics, judgmental and just plain mean. Such is their view of God, and such is their way of treating others.

But mercy and kindness are fundamentals of the Christian faith. The fruits of the Spirit are "Love, joy, peace, forbearance, kindness, goodness, faithfulness" (Galatians 5 NIV).

Where do you fit in this regard? Are you filled with these fruits? For your benefit, I am including my analysis of "agape love," later on in this book, as well. Please read it and decide where you stand, and if your rigidity overpowers these fruits, it's time to ask God for help.

13. SPICE UP YOUR SEX LIFE—BUT NOT WITH PORNOGRAPHY

So things are getting sexually monotonous and

you have turned to erotica to stimulate your fantasies. A foolish move, indeed!

If you're a Christian, you should have known that looking at another man/woman to lust after him/her is a sin, and that that makes you guilty before God. You have mentally betrayed your mate and, as a result, your mate is no longer as appealing and attractive to you.

Well, what did you expect? Do you really think Satan would get you to sin without consequences? You lust after those very seductive men or women; you are now obsessed with <u>them</u> and now your mate appears downright unappealing.

If you're not a Christian, and you don't believe in the concept of sin, know that the same consequences apply to your mind as well. Pornography will make you obsessed with other people, and your mate — the one you felt so close to in the past — has now lost appeal and value.

Christian or not, when moving into pornography both groups are looking for greener pastures. But are there really greener pastures out there?

Did you forget that what you see on the screen are actors, and that what you see in the porn magazines or the Internet are posed and "photo-shopped" images that have nothing to do with reality? The bliss they act out is all fake and those super-beautiful ladies and handsome men probably go from partner to partner sexually; or may be simply super narcissists who may be impossible to live with in real life. It's all fantasy and nothing more.

Before you leave your mate to look for someone who will make you taste heaven, as pornography implies, reconsider. Heaven may be in the arms of the man or woman who dedicated his or her life to you. Heaven is beside the one who has been faithful to you and loves you, in spite of your imperfections. Don't leave what you have for a dream that is bound to turn into a horrible nightmare.

Others have — many others — and have lived to regret it.

14. LISTENING: A POWERFUL TOOL

Talkers want to be heard. They think they have much to give to the world, and they expect others to listen—<u>to them</u>. They have no space for others, and if others attempt to speak, they will quickly interrupt.

Speaking and not listening is a curse in all relationships. Not listening frustrates partners and gives them the impression that the mate is selfish and that they don't count.

There is great power in listening—much more that a bunch of foolish talking which often only helps to infuriate our mate.

When your mate has something to say, let him or her talk —*and don't interject*. If he or she is angry— *let him or her vent*. There is ample time to talk. LISTEN!

If you do, the person will feel respected, appreciated, and he/she will have the opportunity to listen to him or her talk, which often ends up showing them that they have been insensitive and unreasonable. Because, you see, oftentimes when people talk, they tend to listen to themselves as well.

If you listen, you will have an opportunity to hear how you are affecting the other person and that the other person is hurting. And this is critical.

The person in front of you is a human being with feelings and sensitivities. That person may be hurting a lot. If you are busy interjecting, contradicting and thinking about what to say next, how in the world can you understand what the other person is saying? Get the point?

The royal way to get a mate to calm down is to let them vent—<u>without interruptions</u>! Can you see the benefits? The person across from you will feel respected; he/she will calm down and then you can have a rational discussion.

Listening is a wonderful tool. <u>Use it!</u>

P.S. In this regard I would like to strongly recommend a brief and very powerful book which has had a transforming power on myself and many others for decades. It is titled, *To Understand Each Other*, by Paul Tournier.

15. NAME CALLING: A LETHAL WEAPON

So you think that using terms such as, "idiot," "retard," "dumb," etc. when you're angry is going to help anything? <u>These terms are poison.</u> You are affecting the other person's self-esteem; you are chiseling away at their self-respect; you are in fact *de-motivating* your mate.

So everyone uses those terms? <u>Everyone who does is wrong!</u> Human beings need seeds of worth planted in their minds—not seeds of worthlessness.

A mate is supposed to build not destroy.

Jesus Christ told us that if we call someone else a fool or an empty head (stupid), we are in serious spiritual danger (Matthew 5:22). Why? Because we are damaging the mind of the other person — and that damage can last a lifetime.

Calling people nasty names is not a demonstration of love, nor does it elicit love from the other person in return. We like people who make us feel good. We love people who think the world of us. Do you want to be loved? Then, be loving with actions—<u>and with words.</u>

16. AFFECTION: THE HEALING BALM

In North America, affection tends to be frowned upon. Kisses, caresses, hugs tend to be given sparingly. I have known spouses that were starving for affection, and the mate refused to see it, or respond.

Affection cannot simply be a prelude to sex—<u>it must be ever present.</u> There are no excuses for being frugal with affection. The fact that your parents were frugal with you is no reason to starve your mate with something so critical.

<u>Love is a need.</u> The famous psychologist Abraham Maslow told us so long ago in his classic Pyramid of Human Needs. <u>A need!</u> And if that need is not satisfied, the hunger will multiply; as will frustration, depression, resentment and finally the temptation to seek it elsewhere.

<u>Do not be sparing with hugs</u>. Give them often and make them long and tight.

<u>Do not be sparing with kisses</u>. Give them often—<u>and sincerely</u>.

<u>Especially, do not be sparing with saying, "I love you;"</u> and say it *from the heart*.

The rewards will be nothing short of amazing for both the man and the woman.

17. GRATITUDE: THE ENERGIZER

Are you taking your mate for granted? Are you

men taking your wife's sacrifices for granted? Are you women taking your husbands' sacrifices for granted? Big mistake!

Lack of gratitude is a great sin and carries great risks, as it spells lack of appreciation.

Your wife may be slaving away all day looking after demanding children. Does she feel appreciated? Are you telling her that she is? She needs to know, be it with an occasional note or with sincere spoken words—or both.

Is your husband holding two jobs to pay the bills and the mortgage? Is he working long hours to be a provider? He needs to know you appreciate what he is doing, verbally or with an occasional note.

Are we sinning this great sin? It is now time to repent and to show gratitude. The results will be a happier, more motivated mate—a wonderful consequence to simply showing appreciation.

18. DON'T BELIEVE EVERYTHING YOU SEE

Satan uses anything he can to influence as many people as he can to let go and start anew. The message is, "You can do better," "Your life can be a lot happier," "Look at the people you know who divorced. See how happy they are?" That may be the case, but don't fool yourself. You may be dealing with the exception, not the rule—and what you see and hear <u>may not be reality at all.</u>

Not many people want to admit that they failed *again.* Lots of people put on a great show and make it seem that all is great, when the reality is quite different.

I learned this lessons many years ago with a family that on the surface appeared to be totally and absolutely perfect. The husband and the wife appeared to be living a perennial nirvana — but it was a gigantic lie, acted for the onlookers —<u>but far from true</u>.

The reality was that the family was a house of horrors. Once I got to know the members of the family separately, the terrible truth came out, and the truth was the total opposite of what I had originally seen.

Beware!

19. BEWARE OF BITTER FRIENDS

There are lots of people out there who hate the opposite sex, because of a failed relationship. In some cases the marital relationship entailed abuse and/or betrayal. These kinds of experiences lead to anger and bitterness, which is often transferred to all members of the human race that happen to be of the same sex as the former mate. Unfortunately, some such people go on a crusade to embitter others as well.

I saw this dynamic once in a work location. A female colleague who had a bad marriage and a painful divorce, and who overflowed with bitterness, did her best to poison the marital relationship of another female colleague who had a decent, though not perfect marriage.

I saw the satanic ploy evolve for quite some time and finally intervened by having a private talk with the married lady the bitter friend was trying hard to poison. I helped her to see what was happening and encouraged her to look at the good things she had going for her, and not to allow anyone to destroy her marriage and potentially her two children.

Fortunately, she did not allow the ploy to impact

her and is, as of today, many years later still happily married with two very fine children.

Beware of bitter divorcees! Beware of bitter human beings that love to share their bitterness with others.

Bitterness has a way of poisoning others around us, as even the Apostle Paul warned: *"Looking diligently lest any man fail of the grace of God; lest any root of bitterness springing up trouble you, and thereby many be defiled" (Hebrews 12:15 KJV).*

Be on guard, therefore—and fight back! The other person may not like you for doing so, but who needs such people around, when they only want to cause you and your family harm?

20. REMEMBER: YOUR CHILDREN ARE WATCHING AND LEARNING

Much of what our children adopt as behaviors comes from us parents. We are their main role models, and even though they may seem to rebel and depart from our standards when they enter the teen years, as they move along in life they have a way of becoming more and more like us parents.

What we model as parents: our way of communicating, our way of dealing with difficult times, *if we are quitters or fighters*; all gets chiseled into their minds and will, in many cases, become their way of dealing with life and relationships.

It is no secret that men and women who come from broken homes have a greater probability of divorcing than fellow humans who come from intact homes. Of course there are other factors, but a major factor is what was modeled for them by their parents.

If they witnessed abuse, they have a high probability — though not necessarily — of becoming abusers. If they witnessed an unwillingness to fight for the marriage, some will quit early—<u>and not even try</u>.

What are they witnessing in your present relationship?

If you are planning to quit without putting up a good fight to save your marriage, in the future they might do the same.

Is that what you want?

21. GIVE HONEY BEFORE CORRECTION

We all make mistakes and are, on occasion, in need of being corrected. There is one proven way that makes correction more palatable and that is giving honey first, before dishing out any correction.

If you first mention something positive to your mate, then he/she will be more willing to accept the correction. Giving only correction tends to get most people on the defensive, and of creating a counter offensive. If, on the other hand, something positive and encouraging is mentioned first, the human mind becomes more receptive.

Too many fights begin with a correction. A series of corrections is finally bound to create resentment and, finally, a negative response. Changing our approach may take some getting used to, as corrections are all too often motivated by irritations.

Jumping immediately into a correction when we feel upset and irritated is very easy to do, but the results are rarely positive, given the human proclivity to want to defend our self-esteem.

Changing approach may require a level of self-control we may not be used to exercising, but the results are worth the effort.

22. PRAY DAILY FOR YOUR MATE

This is a very powerful principle. Prayer works and prayer can change people. I have seen it do wonders in relationships. But prayer for one's mate must be consistent and sincere. Prayer should also include prayers of gratitude for the positive traits in one's mate and the opportunity to be a blessing in his/her life. If you have not done so regularly, ask God daily to help your mate in whatever way he/she requires. Persevere in prayer and, over time, you will see wonderful results.

23. SUPPORT YOUR MATE PUBLICLY

One of the unfortunate things that I have seen

men and women do over the years has been putting their mate down in public. Some do it jokingly; some have been intentionally downright cutting and hurtful. There is nothing to be gained by doing so. Such behavior risks producing resentment in the mate and could lead to increased friction and disrespect.

When in public, speak positively of your mate. Doing so is a public applause, and it will be amply appreciated.

24. SUPPORT YOUR MATE IN FRONT OF YOUR CHILDREN

If you have children, there will be times when they will need correction. Whether you agree with your mate or not, do not contradict your mate in front of the children. Doing so will produce resentment in your mate and it will embolden the children to be rebellious. A united front makes parents strong and much more effective.

If you do disagree with your mate, <u>do so privately</u>. This approach will be respected by your mate and will not affect the children negatively.

25. BE THE SOOTHING BALM AFTER A STRESSFUL DAY

If your mate comes home stressed out, please let him/her do whatever he/she needs to unwind and to recharge. If he or she needs to withdraw for one hour and sit in front to the computer, so be it. Listen to your mate long and hard about their frustrations. Do not judge and do not condemn. Just listen and then do the following:

26. MASSAGES ARE A TOKEN OF LOVE

When your mate is stressed out, stand behind him/her and massage his/her shoulders. Stress produces a lot of tension in the shoulders. If you feel rock-hard muscles that will tell you that your mate is going through a rough time. Massage those muscles with love and you will be adored for doing it.

27. RESPECT THE DIFFERENCES

Men are men and women are not men. We have been created quite different. DO NOT expect men to be sensitive like women, and men DO NOT expect women to be rough and tough like you.

Respect your mate's differences. Accept your mate's differences. You know what they are.

Men are truly from Mars and Women are definitely from Venus; but both are masterpieces made by the Great Master, and He makes no inferior quality products.

Both men and women have special qualities that are supposed to blend and produce a complete and effective "team." A united, harmonious team will be very strong and effective. There is no need to compete; but there is a need to cooperate and to use the differences to create strength.

Couples that have learned to do so are strong couples. You can be the same.

28. PUT YOUR MATE ON A VERY HIGH PEDESTAL

The more we feel valued by a person, the more we love and appreciate that person. The more you value your mate, the more he/she will love and appreciate you. The more we devalue our mate the more we contribute to resentment and, finally, even hatred.

We know where we stand in our mate's eyes. We know if we are special to them or not. Attitudes and words continually reveal where we stand.

If you become determined to put your mate on a very high pedestal, and to value him/her greatly, the benefits will be great for your mate who will be greatly energized, and for you who will be greatly loved in return.

29. LOVE YOUR MATE AS LIFE TRANSFORMS HIM/HER

It has been said that there are two sure things in life: death and taxes. Well, there is one more thing and it's *change*. Life moves on inexorably, and it transforms us—physically and mentally.

There is nothing we can do to change that.

Our appearance will change; our personality will change somewhat, and there is little we can do about it. But there is much we can do in the way we respond.

In time your mate will look different. The beauty of youth will disappear. The energy and vitality will wane. Hormonal changes will bring about mood changes. Health problems will bring about sexual performance issues. A loving and mature person will respond with understanding and support. A selfish and immature person will be judgmental, critical and unsupportive.

As the changes happen, who we really are comes through, and how much we really value the other person shows through as well.

As life brings about the painful changes, it is time to show that we are really men and women of maturity, and, most of all, it is time to show our mate that we love him/her for who they are, and not for how they look.

30. BE A PILLAR OF STRENGTH FOR YOUR MATE WHEN DEATH TAKES LOVED ONES AWAY

Death will come our way, and it will steal from us the ones we love. When this happens in our mate's life, this is a challenging time for them. This is the time to show them vast amounts of support. This is the time to accept and respect their grieving. Some react to the death of a loved one way, some the other. Whatever is your mate's way of grieving, let them grieve—<u>and support them.</u>

For some the grieving process takes a long time. So be it. Be with them *and be patient*. Your love and patience will not be forgotten and will be amply reciprocated, when your time to grieve will come as well.

31. DIVORCE WILL NOT NECESSARILY SOLVE YOUR PROBLEMS

Countless many have chosen divorce as a solution to their marital problems. What they didn't consider — or chose to ignore — is the fact that people who divorce have a greater probability of divorcing the second time around — and the statistics are scary for those who remarry a third time.

The above should not surprise a sensible mind. A person who chooses to deal with marital problems by escaping will have no difficulty doing the same thing next time around. That is the risk of running away from problems, instead of resolving them.

And what about the children? Children of divorced and remarried couples tend to be more aggressive and more depressed. They tend to have more learning problems and more mental illness. They also have more children born out of wedlock and they tend to divorce more than their peers who come from intact families.

This can be validated from a quick Google search. Having also been a high-school teacher and guidance counselor, I can assure you that many teens who come from broken homes tend to be discouraged, irritable, unfocused and provide the most headaches for teachers.

Is this what you want for your children?

Now let's be clear: if you and your children are in danger, or if there is a level of abuse which is inhumane and the mate refuses to confront and address the problem, then it's best to depart and come back only when you are sure you that there is no potential physical or psychological harm and that you and the children are safe.

Outside of such or other extreme circumstances, before divorcing your mate, you should consider the consequences, as they are many—and painful.

CONCLUSION

I hope that what I have given you so far has stimulated some thought, which will lead to positive changes. You might say at this point, "But, Mike, it takes two to tango." True, it does, but one can be a good place to start.

It may, indeed, be true that the cause to your troubles may be your mate; but it may also be true that it could be you, or both.

If the problem is your mate, you may want to

encourage your him or her to read this book and ponder. If the problem is you, and you had not seen it yet, hopefully this book will lead you to consider some critical changes. If it's both, it would be wonderful if both of you could read each point and discuss it together.

Sometimes the only person you can change is yourself. Perhaps, that's what this book will accomplish—and that is no small thing.

As stated in the Introduction, your changes can bring about a change in the negative cycle you and your mate may be in and, thus, some or many positive changes may ensue in your mate as well. Keep on reinforcing the positive cycle and do your best not to add to the negative one. You may be amazed at the results.

My heartfelt wish is that this book has given you some hope, and that you will move on with a renewed sense that though the marriage building is severely damaged much can be done to repair it.

May the Almighty accompany you and strengthen you, as you strive to heal the wounds and rebuild that which was torn down.

Michael Caputo (Minister, counselor, educator)

ADDENDUMS

In this section I will include two areas that are fundamental to failure or success in marriage, but from a biblical perspective.

If you are a Christian, you will be familiar with "The Works of the Flesh" and "The Fruits of the Spirit" listed in Galatians 5.

The Works of the Flesh are the signs of a selfish and carnal mind who disregards God and humans. The "work" I will explore for your benefit is "adultery." The section is extracted from my e-book/paperback, *The Works of the Flesh*, which you may buy on Amazon.

"The Fruits of The Spirit" are traits which indicate a spiritual mind—a mind that is filled with love and concern for others. The "fruit" I will discuss for your benefit will be "agape Love," a fruit that can lead to certain success in marriage. This is a chapter from my book titled, *The Fruits of the Spirit,* presently available on Amazon.

ADULTERY: A WORK OF THE FLESH

Unless otherwise indicated, Bible quotations are taken from the New King James Version. Copyright © 1982 by Thomas Nelson, Inc.

Every single day, Satan brings marital relationships to a painful end, by using a weapon that has been most effective since the beginning of time: adultery.

The consequences to adultery are great anguish for the betrayed, shame for the betrayer and turmoil and confusion for countless innocent children. Satan watches the suffering he causes humanity and rejoices—every single day.

GOD'S PERSPECTIVE

From the beginning God knew, all too well, the horrific consequences that adultery would have had on humanity and, thus, He forbad it in the

Ten Commandments.

> *"Thou Shalt not Commit adultery"* (Ex. 20:14 KJV)

To God marriage is holy and the union between man and women is sacred. Adultery turns that which is holy into something unholy; that which is sacred into something profane.

God made another stern pronouncement about adultery, in the book of Leviticus.

> *[10] If a man commits adultery with another man's wife—with the wife of his neighbor—both the adulterer and the adulteress are to be put to death.* (Leviticus 20:10 NIV).

In the New Testament, the message is exactly the same.

> *Marriage is honorable among all, and the bed undefiled; but fornicators and adulterers God will judge* (Hebrews 13:4).

Thus, Paul *totally* supports the Old Testament teaching that marriage is holy and that polluting it invites God's wrath.

According to *the Journal of Marital and Family Therapy*, the percent of marriages where one or both spouses admit to either physical or emotional infidelity is 41%. The number of men who have strayed at least once in their married life is 22%. The number of women who strayed, at least once, is 14%.i

OPEN TO ADULTERY

The most worrisome revelation, according to the above journal is that 74% of men and 68% of women said *they would* have an affair, if they knew they would never get caught.

This is clearly an indication that American men and women are quite open to mental adultery and that lusting after other men or women has become quite common. Since this is common, in time so will the probability of actually becoming involved in an adulterous relationship, which will, in all too many cases, lead to catastrophic consequences.

WHERE DO WE FIT?

How are *we* doing in this regard? Are *we* clean? What about mental adultery? Could it be that *our* mind is filled with *mental* adultery, like most American men and women seem to be? If so, Christ made it clear that even mental adultery was unacceptable.

> *You have heard that it was said to those*

> *of old, "You shall not commit adultery."* [28] *But I say to you that whoever looks at a woman to lust for her has already committed adultery with her in his heart* (Matthew 5:27-28).

Do we have lustful eyes? Do we lust after women or men on TV? On the Internet?

Men are visually driven. That is one of the well-established differences between men and women. Men are attracted by skin; the more skin is exhibited the more the male mind wants to look—and lust. Some women are attracted visually as well, but, overall, women tend not to be attracted by skin as much as men.

WHAT ABOUT WOMEN?

Christian women need to be aware of this reality. Christian women should dress modestly and not contribute to this problem. That is why skirts should be as close to the knee as possible. Skirts that pull up when sitting will attract men's eyes and it can lead to lust in them.

Low-cut dresses are a problem. Very low-back dresses are a problem as well, though not as much. Very tight skirts can be a problem, as they tend to attract male attention. Very tight pants are a problem as well. The male mind tends to go beyond the pants and immediately visualizes what's under the cloth, thus leading to lust.

In summer, shorts should not be very short. Very short shorts become *exceptionally* short when one bends down. And they should not be very tight either.

Christian women should strive to be conservative with their bathing suits, <u>and so should men</u>, of course.

Shaunti Feldhahn, in her book, *What I Didn't Know About Men*, informs us that "Men are visual." *ii* Yes, men are visual. Christian men have to struggle with this tendency as well—<u>and struggle they must!</u> God expects us to keep our eyes under control and to turn away, as soon as we feel lustful feelings.

Christian men cannot blame women, if they lust. They cannot say, "It's their fault, because they dress seductively." We men must look away, when that is necessary; we must switch channel, when that is required; we must leave the room, if something could lead us to lust.

Christian women are expected to help Christian men in this regard, by making this problem next to nonexistent in the church. Christian women should <u>never</u> be the subject of unwanted attention, because of revealing too much of their bodies.

When it comes to fighting adultery, the best approach is to nip it in the bud. We must be well aware of traps brought to us by Satan.

THE STAGES OF ADULTERY

Adultery doesn't just happen; there are stages that precede it. Before adultery there is the meeting of someone. This leads to liking the someone, which leads to wanting to be around the someone, which leads to infatuation and obsessive thinking about the person, which leads to secret meetings and, finally, the consummation—and then guilt, and then possible addiction to the adultery, and then more guilt, and then moving away from God and His people, and then serious problems within the family, and then fracturing of marriages, and then deep depression and, finally spiritual death, unless repented of.

Women tend to be particularly susceptible to emotional attachments. In fact, some carry on with emotional adultery and never go into the actual adultery. Even so, their heart is alienated from their husbands and, thus, they are mentally in a state of adultery.

It is important to be aware of the steps listed above and to put an end to them, once recognized.

The major key is to ask God *immediately* for help to resist and be delivered from the temptation, or Satan will pull us in, until resisting will be next to impossible.

Proverbs chapter 5 dedicates several verses to warning us about the evils of adultery.

My son, pay attention to my wisdom;

Lend your ear to my understanding,

² That you may preserve discretion,

And your lips may keep knowledge.

³ For the lips of an immoral woman drip honey, And her mouth is smoother than oil; ⁴ But in the end she is bitter as wormwood,

Sharp as a two-edged sword.

⁵ Her feet go down to death,

Her steps lay hold of hell.

⁶ Lest you ponder her path of life—

Her ways are unstable;

You do not know them.

⁷ Therefore hear me now, my children,

And do not depart from the words of my mouth.

⁸ Remove your way far from her,

And do not go near the door of her

house,
⁹ Lest you give your honor to others,
And your years to the cruel one;
¹⁰ Lest aliens be filled with your wealth,
And your labors go to the house of a foreigner;
¹¹ And you mourn at last,
When your flesh and your body are consumed,
¹² And say:
"How I have hated instruction,
And my heart despised correction!
¹³ I have not obeyed the voice of my teachers,
Nor inclined my ear to those who instructed me!
¹⁴ I was on the verge of total ruin,
In the midst of the assembly and congregation."

15 Drink water from your own cistern,

And running water from your own well.

16 Should your fountains be dispersed abroad,

Streams of water in the streets?

17 Let them be only your own,

And not for strangers with you.

18 Let your fountain be blessed,

And rejoice with the wife of your youth.

19 As a loving deer and a graceful doe,

Let her breasts satisfy you at all times;

And always be enraptured with her love.

20 For why should you, my son, be enraptured by an immoral woman,

And be embraced in the arms of a seductress?

21 For the ways of man are before the eyes of the LORD, And He ponders all his paths.

[22] His own iniquities entrap the wicked man,
And he is caught in the cords of his sin.
[23] He shall die for lack of instruction,
And in the greatness of his folly he shall go astray (Proverbs 5:1-23).

The saintly mother gave such a long warning, because she was well aware of the power of sexual temptations on the part of immoral women and wants all men to be proactive and to stay away from such temptresses, when they come across them.

<u>The principle, of course, applies to women as well</u>. There are lots of very seductive, handsome men around who will say and do all it takes to manipulate and seduce naive women, so as to use them sexually and then abandon them to guilt, shame and ruin.

HOW TO PREVENT ADULTERY

Adultery is, therefore, to be evaded. The pulls toward adultery must be fought. The best way to fight adultery is to be proactive. Here are some principles that may help:

1. *We must accept the fact that adultery can happen to each and every one of us.*

We must never think we're immune. Thinking that we are undefeatable would be begging for trouble. The Apostle Paul gives a very sober warning to such people:

> *Therefore let him who thinks he stands take heed lest he fall* (I Corinthians 10:12).

2. *Know that Satan loves this device—because he knows it works.*

Sexual temptations worked with mighty David, and they can work with us as well—<u>and it can happen when we least expect it</u>. Thus, we can safely expect that Satan will most probably try it on us mentally, or in real life. Christians must always be on guard and expect the possibility that Satan may attack at any time.

3. Let's not forget that a person who commits adultery doesn't just betray a mate—he/she betrays God as well.

If a Christian falls to Satan's temptation, he/she will not just abandon his relationship with his or her mate, he/she abandons his or her relationship with God.

The greatest betrayal is of the Father who loves us and the Son who died for our sins.

4. Know for certain that adultery may be

hidden from man, but not from God, and that God, in time, will make it come out in the open.

There are many examples when God made sure that the affair was discovered in the most amazing ways—*even though it may have been hidden with great care.*

5. *Know that a punishment will for certain follow—and, sometimes, it will be drastic.*

There will be mental agony at first in the form of guilt and then depression and anger and, finally, whatever consequence God has in store for the adulterer, which could be quite painful.

> *Marriage is honorable among all, and the bed undefiled; but fornicators and adulterers God will judge"* (Hebrews 13:4).

This implies a firm consequence on God's part, so as to get the adulterer to repent.

6. *Know that adultery, even if it is just mental and emotional, separates from God and, thus, it takes away God's protection and opens the doors to curses—and to attacks from Satan.*

Sin separates from God—and it links us to Satan. When we commit adultery, we move into the Devil's camp, and we become his servants. The enemy will finally reward us with pain, anguish and even disasters.

7. *Know that if we are tolerant of the stages that precede consummation, the rest will be hard to resist.*

Adultery starts in the mind. It starts with

thoughts and emotions. Unless it is caught at the early stages, it will turn into an obsession which will potentially translate into action.

> *For out of the heart proceed evil thoughts, murders, adulteries, fornications, thefts, false witness, blasphemies (Matthew 15:19).*

We, therefore, must fight evil thoughts as they arise, and must do our utmost to prevent them from finding residence in our minds.

> *...and take every thought captive to obey Christ... (2 Corinthians 10:5).*

By so doing, we will not have to fight a more powerful battle later on when the temptation may be a lot harder to resist.

8. Beware of things that contribute to lustful thoughts and to adultery.

TV: Sexually explicit shows, movies and soap operas. Directors intentionally use very attractive and seductive men and women to get watchers to become addicted.

The Internet: A great blessing and a great curse. Way too many Christians have become slaves to pornographic web sites. The Internet has become one of Satan's greatest modern tools. If Christians become addicted, and they don't stop—*the end result can be disastrous.*

Porno Movies: Watching pornographic movies means inviting disaster, even if watched with one's mate. It will invariably lead to lusting and fantasizing about the seductive actor or actress. <u>It is poison!</u>

9. Beware of work. Many affairs take place with people at work.

Meeting new people makes the possibility for adultery greater. As the number of women who enter the work force increases so does the frequency of adultery.

We Christian men and women must be fully aware of this and must always be on guard. If someone is getting too close, we must keep our distance. Make your values evident. <u>Make your commitment evident</u>. Keep your language clean, and wear conservative clothes. By so doing, you will project a clean image.

If you have problems with your mate, know that Satan will provide kind, understanding, loving men or women to entrap you.

Many affairs have started with supportive

friends of the opposite sex, during difficult times. Such friendships can easily deteriorate into strong emotional and, finally, sexual relationships.

Spending much non-work-related time alone with fellow workers of the opposite sex is very risky. It can, in time, lead to adultery—<u>and then disaster</u>.

10. Pray every morning Christ's prayer: "Deliver us from the Evil One."

Why? Because Jesus knew that every day Satan would try to entrap us. God's help is critical to protect us from falling into Satan's well-planned traps.

11. The greater the closeness to God the greater the ability to see danger approaching, and the greater will be the strength to say

"No!" when the temptation comes our way.

Christ's words, *"The flesh is weak"* (Matthew 26:41) is absolutely true and in Satan's hands it becomes especially weak.

Satan uses temptation to get us to commit adultery and we must resist and fight *and persist in the fight* day in and day out.

12. Jesus Christ also gave us the secret to success and it is found in the Gospel of Matthew.

> *Watch and pray, lest you enter into temptation. The spirit indeed is willing, but the flesh is weak (Matthew 26: 41).*

Though the flesh is weak, God's spirit is willing and able to move us to do what is right. It is willing to help us say no, when a man or woman comes our way as Satan's instrument to get us to sin.

WHAT IF YOU HAVE COMMITTED ADULTERY?

If you have committed adultery, and you are a Christian or a person of faith, you have tasted the bitter consequences of this destructive sin. You have tasted the guilt and the shame; you have experienced the negative impact it can have on one's self esteem.

You may have also seen the consequences on your marital relationship and on others around you.

To you God says very simply, "Repent and start anew." If you repent and ask for forgiveness, you will be a new person. If your repentance is sincere, <u>to God you will be totally clean</u>.

Just remember Jesus Christ's words to the woman caught in adultery: "*Go and sin no more*" (John 8:11 KJV).

WHAT IF YOU ARE STILL COMMITTING ADULTERY?

If you are now committing adultery, and you are convinced that your sinful behavior is wrong, and that it must end, <u>wait no longer</u>. It is never too late. God longs to see you stop hurting yourself and others. His words to you are the following:

> *Come now, and let us reason together, saith the Lord: though your sins be as scarlet, they shall be as white as snow; though they be red like crimson, they shall be as wool (Isaiah 1:18 KJV).*

Please listen to His invitation and spare yourself all the anguish that awaits you, if you won't stop.

THE POWERFUL TOOLS AT OUR DISPOSAL

The problem of adultery, therefore, abounds. It is a serious problem with serious consequences. But the solutions abound as well, and they are very simple: prayer, Bible study and fasting.

By having an intimate relationship with God, we are daily energized to fight temptations—<u>and to win</u>. God will provide us with unlimited energy to resist, and, finally, Satan will flee from us, as the Scriptures promise in James 4:7.

They are three barriers that Satan cannot penetrate. They are weapons that the flesh cannot win against.

CONCLUSION

As we have seen, adultery has become a real scourge on society. The consequences are disastrous for the sinner as well as the innocent—especially children.

To fight adultery, it is best to be proactive. We must keep in mind that Satan will attack whenever he can, and that he will use very seductive men and women to get us to sin.

The tools at our disposal are very powerful, but they must be used regularly.

God is on our side, and He will empower those who want to live a holy life. He is also longing to see those who have been trapped by this sin, stop, repent and strive to live a spiritually clean life, once again.

> As Christians, therefore, let us do our utmost, every day, to fulfill God's wish and command:
>
> *Be you holy as I am Holy (I Peter 1:16 NKJV)*

Let's do some serious and honest soul-searching, therefore, and let's do what is our duty to do to win the battle against Satan and one of his most effective weapons: adultery.

LOVE: A FRUIT OF THE SPIRIT

Unless otherwise indicated, Bible quotations are taken from the New King James Version. Copyright © 1982 by Thomas Nelson, Inc.

The importance of love is a fundamental theme in the Bible. Love is the very first "fruit of the Spirit" listed in Galatians 5. But the type of love mentioned in Galatians 5 is a very special kind of love with very special characteristics.

In this article this amazing fruit will be discussed in great depth, so as to give the reader a much more complete understanding of this most fundamental Christian trait. But, before doing so, we must discuss what the fruit of love is not.

There are three Greek words translated "love" in the New Testament. One such word is "eros" which, as the word implies, refers to passionate emotion. It is feeling-based, and it is not necessarily lasting love. It is something the world abounds in. It is a sensual kind of love, and it has no spiritual dimension to it.

Another Greek word which is also translated love is "philia." The word philia refers to having "affection" or "fondness" for someone, be it family or friend. It is used a few times in the New Testament to refer to love for the brethren, and it is translated in both the KJV and the NKJV as "brotherly love." It can also be used to refer to the fondness God has for mankind, the fondness of Christ for the church, but based on my research this word is only used twice in that regard. The word used in the list in Galatians 5 is not philia but "agape."

What is the meaning of agape?

According to *Vine's Dictionary of New Testament Words,* agape (noun) and agapao (verb), as used in the New Testament, mean the following:

> a. To describe the attitude of God to His son, the human race, generally, and to such as believe on the Lord Jesus Christ, particularly.
>
> b. It is also used to convey His will to His children concerning their attitude one to another and toward all men.iii

That is, God wills that His converted children especially love God and one another, and that they love the human race as well.

The Oxford Dictionary of the Christian Church emphasizes that in the New Testament the word agape was used to indicate a volitional kind of love which is naturally expressed by the Creator, but not by humans. It is the kind of self sacrificial love that Christians share with each other and toward unbelievers. iv

Agape Love is mentioned first in the list of the Fruits of the Spirit, because it is the foundation of it all. Love is not only a fruit of the Spirit, it is also the roots, the tree trunk and the branches that produce all the other fruits. Love is the major source of joy, peace, longsuffering, kindness, goodness, faithfulness, gentleness, self-control.

It is also critical that we be reminded of the fact that the Holy Spirit, as we well understand, <u>is God</u>. The Fruits of the Spirit emanate from God. The Scriptures tell us that "God is love" (1 John 4:8). Thus all the fruits emanate from Love—that is from God who is Love.

Our mission is to also become love. We have to

love God and Jesus Christ with all our heart, mind and soul, and we have to love our human brothers and sisters as ourselves.

But how do we do that? How do we express agape toward other human beings? That is the topic of this section: *how does agape love manifest itself?*

I would like to propose to you that agape love manifests itself in two fundamental ways.

The first manifestation of agape is <u>obedience</u>; Obedience to God's commandments, to Jesus Christ's commandments and His apostles' commandments, as inspired by the Holy Spirit.

In the past, some of us gladly and in some cases fanatically embraced the need to obey God's Commandments. As a result, some of us became *very obedient*—rigidly obedient and also self-righteous, proud, superior and judgmental. That is unfortunately what happens when we become fervent and fanatical about obedience, but we are lacking in the second manifestation of agape.

Obedience *was and remains* fundamental to our Christian life. Obedience is a <u>critical part</u> of being good Christians. But some of us stopped there and, by so doing, we stopped growing; for spiritual growth entails commitment to obeying God plus growth in the second area: <u>holy attitudes</u>. True agape, which is poured on us by God, manifests itself in both obedience and agape attitudes. Where there is an abundance of agape, there is love for God's laws and there is an abundance of agape attitudes. <u>Both are present.</u>

Let's call these two aspects, *the two pillars of agape*. Let's therefore review both pillars and let's ask ourselves: Do I manifest a balance between the two areas, or am I only focusing on one and not the other?

PILLAR 1: OBEDIENCE TO GOD'S COMMANDMENTS

Let's first of all look at the first pillar: obedience to God's laws. If we are filled with God's Spirit, we will be moved to obey God's commandments, and we will be empowered to obey God's Commandments.

God, from the beginning to the end of His Word, stresses and demands obedience to His Commandments. Thus He gave us the two great Commandments, and both have to do with Love.

> Deuteronomy 6:5
>
> *Love the LORD your God with all your*

heart and with all your soul and with all your strength. (NIV)

Leviticus 19:18

Do not seek revenge or bear a grudge against one of your people, but love your neighbor as yourself." (NIV)

God clarified these two great commandments further in the Ten Commandments. He also proceeded to give us other important requirements in the Book of the Law. But He didn't stop there. In the New Testament He expanded further on His Commandments through Jesus Christ and, finally, gave more finishing touches with His Apostles.

Lest there not be any doubt as to the necessity of obeying God's Commandments, in the Gospels Christ <u>confirmed</u> the necessity of obeying them.

> *But if thou wilt enter into life, keep the commandments (Matthew 19:17 KJV).*

The Apostles also supported this fundamental truth.

> *Therefore the law is holy, and the commandment holy and just and good" (Romans 7:12).*

> *He who says I know him and does not keep His commandments is a liar and the truth is not in Him (I John 2:4).*

This is our God; a God who loves all of His children deeply and who wants them all treated with respect and dignity. By obeying His commandments we show love and respect toward God's children. This is Agape. This is God's love.

But there is more. As we receive His spirit, new dimensions must be added to our minds that go beyond obedience. That is pillar two. And this is where some of us at times are lacking.

The second manifestation or pillar two is agape attitudes. Obedience without God's attitudes may be a manifestation of *our righteousness*, not necessarily God's righteousness, *which is authored and maintained by God's Spirit.*

How do we know that our righteousness is ours and not God's? Because the following attitudes *will not* accompany it.

PILLAR 2: AGAPE ATTITUDES

1 Corinthians 13 is one of the most beloved chapters in the Bible. It is often quoted, but not necessarily understood. We even read it as the

list of attitudes <u>we</u> ought to implement, when in reality they are attitudes that <u>God must place in us</u>, if they are to be real and lasting.

Let's analyze this most supreme chapter thoroughly.

> *1 Though I speak with the tongues of men and of angels, but have not love, I have become sounding brass or a clanging cymbal...*

Though I have the outward manifestations of spirituality that some take great pride in, but I am not filled with agape, I am nothing. I am an instrument that makes lots of noise but no pleasant sound.

> *2 And though I have the gift of prophecy, and understand all mysteries and all knowledge...*

Though I have been chosen by God Himself to be a prophet, and though I have the deepest understanding of the Scriptures and know Hebrew, Aramaic and New Testament Greek; if I am not filled with agape, I am nothing.

> *and though I have all faith, so that I could remove mountains,*

Though I have tremendous faith to do great things that will leave people stunned by the miracles that I can perform, but have not agape, <u>I am nothing.</u>

> *3 And though I bestow all my goods to feed the poor...*

All my goods to feed the poor. Can there be more agape love than that? Well, not really. Two of the most giving people on earth today are agnostics. They are Bill Gates and Warren

Buffett. They have set up a charitable foundation that is worth billions. It is called the "Bill and Melinda Gates Foundation," now also supported by Warren Buffett.

But is it motivated by agape? Or is it the kind of love that according to Paul gives much and yet is worthless to God? The difference is the source and the motivation.

Why are they doing it? It could be in part because they are kind people (exercising Philia love, which humans can exercise without God's help), it could be in part for tax purposes, or it could be their own monument to themselves.

Some great people of the past have built buildings to their memory, others have built monuments. Today doing that would not be well received. It would be much better received to create a foundation to noble causes worth billions of dollars that would last for decades or even centuries, if the billions are well managed. What better way to be admired, respected and loved. What better way to create a glorious image that will last on and on. What better way to achieve eternity....

One can give everything he/she possesses to charity and do it with the wrong attitude. *These two people have no place for God in their lives; they are God in their own eyes.* They have their worshippers; they have great wealth and power; they can now have eternity through their foundation and their accomplishments. But to God their billions are not enough. They may be impressing men, but God is not necessarily impressed, as Paul reminds us.

> *...and though I give my body to be burned...*

Can there be a greater sacrifice? Not only to give one's life but to offer it as a burnt sacrifice. Isn't that what Muslim terrorists do? Do they not offer their lives to a holy cause? Are they not in their eyes God's holy warriors?

They may offer their bodies to be dismembered, but they do not have agape, and, thus, *it profits them nothing*. How do we know if we are filled with agape love, then? What are the characteristics that indicate its presence?

4 Love suffers long...

Love suffers long. Love is <u>very</u> patient, even when in being patient one is suffering. God is <u>very</u> patient. He waited hundreds of years before intervening with Noah's world, with the Canaanites and thousands before He intervenes and deals with a degenerate humanity. We have to be longsuffering too.

But we are not required to suffer forever. When our mental and physical health is at stake, then we act and do something about the problem—but not with a spirit of vengeance. We wait with God's strength as long as possible and then finally we do something about the problem—<u>but always motivated by love</u>, never motivated by a spirit of vengeance.

Sometimes we have to be longsuffering with a weak spiritual brother or sister. The strength to do so comes from agape.

Christ is longsuffering with us, especially when we go through spiritually weak times. We have to be longsuffering with others, when they are going through a spiritually weak times. We "turn the other cheek," and we bear offences gracefully.

...with all lowliness and gentleness, with

longsuffering, bearing with one another in love...(Ephesians 4:2).

God asks much from us, when He asks us to be this longsuffering. But the key point is not only that we must exercise longsuffering, <u>the key point is we must exercise longsuffering with the love and strength given to us by God, through agape.</u>

We are longsuffering because we use God's strength and we apply God's wisdom to know how to finally deal with the problem.

> *Not rendering evil for evil, or railing for railing: but contrariwise blessing; knowing that ye are thereunto called, that ye should inherit a blessing (1 Peter 3:9 KJV).*

We have been called to endure persecution. The enduring patiently is part of our training to be

God's children. We have to be like God and, thus, we suffer long, with His power, with His patience and with His agape love.

> *Agape is kind...*

True agape-filled Christians are kind people. They show *sincere* kindness, even to people who don't deserve kindness. They give and serve with kindness *and sincerity*.

There are kind people in this world who are not Christians. Some may be kind by nature; some may have learned to be kind from their parents; some choose to be kind. That is "philia" kindness. Some are sincere, some are not. Some simply put on an act. Some act kind to get something in return. It is hard to know.

Some become very kind during Christmas and Easter time and then go back to being unkind for the rest of the year. True agape-filled Christians are not harsh with others—*even if they deserve it.* They even treat their enemies kindly, *and they do it with God's Agape love*. If it is agape kindness, it is God who does it—<u>not us</u>. The praise goes to Him—<u>not us</u>.

> *Agape does not envy...*

In the series on the works of the flesh we saw that envy is one of the manifestations of carnal nature, and that it must be fought and defeated. Agape rejoices in the success of others; it celebrates the success of others.

Our minds are not tortured by comparing ourselves with others. We are content with what God blesses us with, and we don't lust after what is not ours. We have peace, because we don't allow envy to torture us. This is not our doing. <u>This is God's doing</u>.

An American university professor who specializes in the study of happiness stated recently that the unhappiest people are the richest or very materialistic people, because no matter what they have, they always look at what they don't have. We are told that "...*envy is rottenness to the bones*" *(Proverbs 14:30)* and not to envy sinners (Proverbs 23:17).

There are times of want in a Christian's life, and there are also times of plenty that God may choose to bring our way. Whatever comes our way, we accept, and we don't envy people who have more. God will make the times of plenty come when He is ready, *and when we are ready*.

> *Keep your lives free from the love of money and be content with what you have, because God has said, 'Never will I leave you; never will I forsake you'*

(Hebrews 13:5 NIV).

An agape-filled Christian knows and believes this and accepts God's blessings or lack thereof. Most of all, he doesn't compare himself to others. An agape-filled Christian, therefore, is free from envy. And this is another characteristic of God's agape love.

> *Love does not parade itself, is not puffed up...*

A Christian has all the reasons in the world to be puffed up. He has been chosen by God as a "first fruit." He is being trained to rule over cities or nations and over hosts of angels. We have lots of reasons to walk around with our heads up high and a pompous attitude. Agape prevents all that, for agape produces the opposite attitude.

In Christian churches we have the lowly and the strong. We have people with little and some with much. We have people in our church who are very successful by human standards; yet agape prevents them from being puffed up and from being conceited.

We have some people who are honored during the week, because of their positions, who then honor us on the Sabbath by doing menial jobs to serve the congregation.

Jesus Christ told us to wash one another's feet, literally and figuratively. When we serve, we don't parade ourselves; we humble ourselves—if we are motivated by Agape, that is.

Some day we will have all the honor anyone could ever wish for, but for now we keep our head low and our hands busy washing feet any time we can. This is done with the right attitude if motivated by agape love.

Let nothing be done through strife or vainglory; but in lowliness of mind let each esteem other better than themselves (Philippians 2:3).

When we serve someone else we esteem them above ourselves. This is not easy. At the most, human nature might sacrifice and go as far as esteeming others as oneself. Esteeming others in the church as being above ourselves and doing so sincerely is a manifestation of Agape love.

Jesus Christ could have come to earth and could have shown off His power and could have been pompous about it. Jesus Christ, instead, divested Himself of all His glory and came down to earth to live among men, and rather than show off and demand submission — which He could have done — He esteemed humanity above Himself. He did not parade himself, and He was not puffed up.

In fact, when He offered His body to be flagellated and then to be crucified for us, He didn't esteem us as much as himself—<u>He esteemed us above himself.</u> Jesus Christ, on that glorious Passover Day when He offered Himself for us, made an amazing agape statement: "<u>I love you humans more than I love myself.</u>"

That is our God. That is agape love.

> *5 does not behave rudely...*

The world allows, and even celebrates rudeness. North America used to be the land of politeness. TV shows modeled proper actions and proper talk. Have you watched TV lately? Hollywood now commonly models crude and distorted behavior and language. Movies are replete with crude and inappropriate language and behaviors.

Teachers are continually correcting bad manners— in some cases very bad manners. This is the new North America, this is the new world. Hypocritically, many teachers are more crude than many students. I have worked with teachers that use very foul language.

We are told not to follow trends. We are different. Our language has to be clean. We try to be polite. We try to be appropriate and respectful. On occasion we stumble. We feel sorry and try harder next time. But our mission is to be sincerely polite at all times. As we grow in agape love, our politeness multiplies, for that is a manifestation of God's mind—<u>of His love</u>.

---

does not seek its own...

This world is saturated with selfishness. No matter how much people seem to be on our side, one has to always watch what they are up to.

Selfishness abounds in all areas of society. We are told that in the last days people will be lovers of their own selves. That time is here, now.

Unlike the world, agape-filled Christians are *altruists.* We are givers, from the heart. If we are motivated by agape, we don't put on a show; we don't serve to be liked, and we don't serve to reach a position.

We give, when possible, without being seen. We don't give so that a wing of a hospital will be named after us; so that our name will be posted on a wall; so that a Foundation will be named after us; so that a speech will be given to honor us; so that we'll get a certificate or a plaque or a trophy. We give because that is what flows from God into us and out toward others. The trophy belongs to God—not to us.

I have heard of some Christians in the past who brought shopping to other needy Christians homes and left it on their veranda. They rang their bell and left. This is agape love. That is what we read in Matthew 6:4.

> *That your alms may be in secret: and thy Father which sees in secret himself shall reward thee openly* (Matthew 6:4 KJV).

Agape love gives without wanting credit for it. But this requires a word of caution: We can fool ourselves that because we give in secret we are exercising agape love. It may not necessarily be the case. We may give in secret to feel spiritually superior, because we give in secret.

If giving in secret makes us feel spiritually superior to others, then it's not agape love, it's mental games that we play with ourselves to feel superior to others. "The human mind is deceitful above all things," we are told in Jeremiah 17:9, and it can deceive us in this regard as well.

Agape love gives in secret and does not feel superior. <u>It is true, pure and holy love</u>.

> *is not (easily) provoked...*

Sometimes people try to provoke us on purpose. They test us. They stir us up to get us to react. Agape will not relent. We all have been around people who try to get us to stop acting nice. It could be relatives; it could be neighbors; it could be fellow workers; it could be students, if you are a teacher. Agape does not relent. We react appropriately, given the occasion, and we will not allow them to get the best of us.

Now, notice it doesn't say that we are not ever provoked. It says that we are not "easily provoked." If they persist in provoking us, we will finally act, but without losing control; without being rude; without being harsh; without causing harm—*without ever being vengeful*.

The Apostle Paul, you may recall, finally appealed to Caesar. The Law is there for our protection. Authorities are there for our benefit.

Agape gives us the strength not to be easily provoked, but after having waited and waited for a prolonged period of time, we can, finally, address the situation legally and appropriately— <u>but not vengefully</u>.

It's called agape love.

> *thinks no evil...*

There are various translations for this expression.

The New American Standard Version: "...does not take into account a wrong suffered."

The Amplified Bible: "It takes no account of the evil done to it (it pays no attention to a suffered wrong)."

The New International Version: "It keeps no record of wrongs."

Clearly this is not an easy section to translate, and it may be because the package included is quite big. We can summarize by saying that the expression means all of the following: We are not to think evil; we are not to rejoice in evil; we are not to keep records of evil as we have to be forgiving.

In short, our relationship with evil has to be a distant one, *and we are not to allow evil to make us become evil*, as keeping a record of evil makes us bitter and resentful—and thus evil. As Romans 12:21 (KJV), warns us: *"Be not overcome of evil, but overcome evil with good."* It takes a special kind of power to fulfill this requirement. It takes Agape to fulfill this requirement. This is what Paul is saying. If you are filled with agape, you will not be overcome of evil, and you will overcome evil with good.

It's agape love.

> *6 does not rejoice in iniquity...*

People who are agape filled do not rejoice in seeing, or hearing about evil. We do not enjoy violence in movies, nor do we rejoice when vengeance takes place in movies. We have an aversion to anything evil, and we try to evade it. And that includes entertainment.

> *but rejoices in the truth...*

True Christians rejoice in being around people who are truthful. We celebrate sincerity, and we try to be sincere. We follow our Master's example that could have lied His way out of death, but told the truth until the end—*even if it meant death*.

We follow the examples of the apostles who could have lied their way out of several very dangerous circumstances, but did not and, instead, bore whippings, beatings and humiliations of all kinds, because they stayed faithful to truth until the end.

To be truthful, at times, takes great courage. Agape love makes it flow out of us naturally, no matter the consequences.

A lying spirit is not from God. Lying effortlessly indicates the presence of Satan's spirit. Lying to get out of trouble indicates spiritual weakness. If that is the case, we need to fill up with agape love.

> *7 bears all things...*

Agape is longsuffering. Again, doubly emphasized. If it is emphasized twice, it's because it's important. It's also very hard, and it can only be accomplished with God's help.

> *believes all things ...*

That is, believes all things that come from God. This is not saying that we believe anything that anyone tells us, for naïve we are not. Paul did not believe Cretans, as he himself said they were liars and could not be trusted. We believe all of God's promises, but are weary of human nature, and stay on guard with human beings.

> *hopes all things...*

It longs for the promises of God and knows that God will keep His promises, in this life and in the future. It believes that all things work for our best and knows that, even the greatest trial, good results await us in the end.

> *endures all things.*

It endures any trial and persecution that their Christian life brings their way—because of the strength given to them by God.

> 8 Love never fails.

Agape never fails. What a stunning promise. The way of agape will <u>always</u> work...it will never fail. *Agape will always produce the best results.*

Paul then concludes:

> *But whether there are prophecies, they will fail; whether there are tongues, they will cease; whether there is knowledge, it will vanish away. 9 For we know in part and we prophesy in part.*
>
> *10 But when that which is perfect has come, then that which is in part will be done away.*
> *11 When I was a child, I spoke as a child, I understood as a child, I thought as a child; but when I became a man, I put away childish things. 12 For now we see in a mirror, dimly, but then face to face. Now I know in part, but then I shall know*

> *just as I also am known. 13 And now abide faith, hope, love, these three; <u>but the greatest of these is love</u>.*

The greatest of all is God's self-sacrificial love that is totally pure, totally sincere and motivated by nothing else but the pure Love of God. The love that manifests itself in the keeping of God's Commandments, in the attitudes listed in I Corinthians 13 and in service to one another and to the human race. <u>A perfect package that never fails.</u>

In the past we have seen people in the church who operated well at the "don't do" level. *They didn't do.* They kept the Commandments perfectly—<u>or so they thought they did</u>.

But Commandment keeping is not necessarily a manifestation of agape love. It may be simply a form of pride or a form of showing off one's superiority over others. Such a person becomes filled with self-righteousness and is harsh and critical of others.

This is what happens when obedience is not tempered with agape; when it's not the result of agape.

Agape is the cap stone. Agape is the energy that drives everything. Agape is the force that motivates "true" obedience, for one can obey out of fear, out of duty, *or out of agape*—the love that proceeds from God. When agape is the heart and core of it all, everything is in perfect balance and the result is nothing short of wonderful.

> *Therefore, as the elect of God, holy and beloved, put on tender mercies, kindness, humility, meekness, longsuffering; 13 bearing with one another, and forgiving one*

another, if anyone has a complaint against another; even as Christ forgave you, so you also must do. 14 But above all these things put on love (agape), <u>which is the bond of perfection</u> (Colossians 3:12-14 NKJV).

True perfection comes from God. It is authored by God and it is energized and maintained by the love of God. When we stay close to God in prayer, Bible study, fasting and meditation, we get filled with agape.

Over the years, if we stay close to God, we become saturated with agape, *and, finally, at the resurrection we will become agape...as God is agape.*

When that amazing event will finally happen, obedience to God's will become effortless. God's attitudes will emanate from us naturally, effortlessly and abundantly.

Until then, though, we must stay close to God daily. We must plug ourselves in daily and abundantly and, by so doing, we will experience a gradual but certain transformation from beings that were filled with selfishness before conversion to beings that tried to produce Philia love, after conversion; to beings that became filled with agape love, over time, by being close to God; to beings that became agape love, at the resurrection.

That is the future; that is what we long for: to become agape as God is agape and to share that love with God, Jesus Christ, our spiritual brothers and sisters and all the angels for eternity.

Let's grow in agape love therefore. Let's be filled with it. Let's become like the God of agape more and more very day. Let's, most of all, long for the day when we will become agape as God is agape.

MICHAEL CAPUTO'S BOOKS ON AMAZON

BIBLE PROPHECIES

The Great Tribulation: How to Escape, or Survive the Great, Future, Worldwide Catastrophe—and Not Be a Traitor

False Prophets and the Antichrist

Seven Lessons From the Seven Churches in Revelation

The Churches of Philadelphia and Laodicea in Revelation: Two Attitudes; Two Destinies

Why Does the Lord Jesus Delay His Coming?

INSPIRATIONAL

What Will Christian Do For Eternity? The Ten Phases of Eternity

Jesus Christ: A Personal Autobiography

The Apostle Paul: How Did the Great Apostle Endure Persecutions, Abuse and Other Great Trials? (KINDLE/PAPERBACK)

When Suffering, Persecutions and Tribulations Come Your Way (KINDLE/PAPERBACK)

We Believe! The Greatest Minds Believed in God (Kindle/paperback)

The Young King and the Cross

Einstein, Galileo, Newton: What Did the Greatest Scientists Believe About God?

ANSWERING THE CRITICS OF CHRISTIANITY

Is God Cruel?: An In-Depth Analysis of God's Apparent Acts of Cruelty in the Bible (KINDLE/PAPERBACK)

God and Catastrophes: When Catastrophes Hit Humanity, Where is God?

Was Jesus Christ Really Resurrected? An Objective Analysis of the Compelling Evidence

The Ten Commandments: Great Proofs of God's

Existence

CHRISTIAN LIVING

The Works of the Flesh: Understanding and Defeating the Works of the Devil (KINDLE/PAPERBACK)

"Be You Holy": How to Grow in God's Holiness in an Unholy World

MISCELLANEOUS

Human Nature: Good, Neutral or Evil? A Biblical Perspective on the Nature of Man

SUGGESTED FREE LITERATURE FROM UCG.ORG

(No Follow up)

http://www.ucg.org/booklets/

WORKS CITED

i *Associated Press, Journal of Marital and Family Therapy.* In *Statistic Brain web site*. <http://www.statisticbrain.com/infidelity-statistics> (22-03-2013).

ii Feldhahn, Shaunti. "For Women Only: What You Need to Know about the Inner Lives of Men," *Mulnomah Publishers.* <http://shop.cbn.com/firstchapter.asp?mode=view&index=577> (15-03-2013).

iii. W. E. Vine, *Vine's Expository Dictionary of New Testament Words*.

iv. F. L. Cross, E. A. Livingstone, *The Oxford Dictionary of the Christian Church*.

Made in the USA
Lexington, KY
11 September 2019